IF FOUND PL]

👤 _____

✉ _____

📱 _____

Greater Than a Tourist Book Series Reviews from Readers

I think the series is wonderful and beneficial for tourists to get information before visiting the city.

-Seckin Zumbul, Izmir Turkey

I am a world traveler who has read many trip guides but this one really made a difference for me. I would call it a heartfelt creation of a local guide expert instead of just a guide.

-Susy, Isla Holbox, Mexico

New to the area like me, this is a must have!

-Joe, Bloomington, USA

This is a good series that gets down to it when looking for things to do at your destination without having to read a novel for just a few ideas.

-Rachel, Monterey, USA

BOOK DESCRIPTION

Are you excited about planning your next trip?

Do you want to try something new?

Would you like some guidance from a local?

If you answered yes to any of these questions, then this Greater Than a Tourist book is for you.

Greater Than a Tourist- Adelaide, South Australia by Nadya Siapin offers the inside scoop on Adelaide. Most travel books tell you how to travel like a tourist. Although there is nothing wrong with that, as part of the Greater Than a Tourist series, this book will give you travel tips from someone who has lived at your next travel destination.

In these pages, you will discover advice that will help you throughout your stay. This book will not tell you exact addresses or store hours but instead will give you excitement and knowledge from a local that you may not find in other smaller print travel books.

Travel like a local. Slow down, stay in one place, and get to know the people and the culture. By the time you finish this book, you will be eager and prepared to travel to your next destination.

TABLE OF CONTENTS

BOOK DESCRIPTION
TABLE OF CONTENTS
DEDICATION
ABOUT THE AUTHOR
HOW TO USE THIS BOOK
FROM THE PUBLISHER
OUR STORY
WELCOME TO
> TOURIST
INTRODUCTION
1. Why Visit Adelaide
2. How To Get Around
3. What Side Of The Road To Drive On
4. Places To Stay
5. Places To Shop
6. Glenelg Is More Than Jetty Road
7. Parking At Glenelg
8. Visit Henley Beach
9. Spend A Day At Semaphore
10. Parking Garages
11. Say G'day, Mate
12. Sun Survival
13. Attractions In The City
14. Best Place For Nightlife

15. Buying Souvenirs
16. Check Out The Chocolate Factories
17. Drive The Adelaide Hills
18. Things To Watch Out For While Driving
19. Wildlife Parks And Sanctuaries
20. Places To Drink
21. Places To Eat
22. Sweet Cravings
23. Local Cuisine To Try
24. Should You Tip
25. Shopping Hours
26. Visit The Barossa Valley
27. Drive To McLaren Vale
28. Take A Drive To Victor Harbor
29. See Port Adelaide
30. See The Botanic Gardens
31. Morialta Conservation And Recreation Park
32. The Best Walking Trails Around Adelaide
33. Local Fishing Charters
34. Top Fishing Spots
35. Best Beaches For Surfing
36. Best Beaches For Snorkelling And Diving
37. Best Places To Rent Underwater Gear
38. The Best Way To See Dolphins
39. Safety At The Beach
40. The Best Festivals

41. Must See Museums
42. The Best Time To Visit
43. How To Use Roundabouts
44. Basic Bushwalking Safety Tips
45. Spider Safety Tips
46. Conserve The Water
47. Remember To Stay Hydrated
48. Dealing With Mosquitoes
49. Common Colloquialisms
50. 'No Shoes, No Shirt, No Service,' Not Exactly

TOP REASONS TO BOOK THIS TRIP
50 THINGS TO KNOW ABOUT PACKING LIGHT FOR TRAVEL
Packing and Planning Tips
Travel Questions
Travel Bucket List
NOTES

>TOURIST

DEDICATION

This book is dedicated to my family and friends, whose brains I picked to get the best ideas.

ABOUT THE AUTHOR

Nadya is a traveler and freelance writer who lives in Adelaide. She loves to kick back at a great café and sample the menu with a book in hand.

Nadya's love of travel has taken her to Europe and on multiple trips between Adelaide and the US, where she was born. She prefers the simple way to travel, carrying her bedroom on her back, and thinks that tenting it is the only way to go.

She's been living in Australia since her family immigrated in 2001. Finishing high school in Adelaide dropped her in the deep end as far as culture and slang go. Now, Adelaide is her permanent address, though she often takes off to see new places. When she's home, she likes to explore the city with fresh eyes, trying new things and wandering down those little side streets.

HOW TO USE THIS BOOK

The Greater Than a Tourist book series was written by someone who has lived in an area for over three months. The goal of this book is to help travelers either dream or experience different locations by providing opinions from a local. The author has made suggestions based on their own experiences. Please do your own research before traveling to the area in case the suggested places are unavailable.

FROM THE PUBLISHER

Traveling can be one of the most important parts of a person's life. The anticipation and memories that you have are some of the best. As a publisher of the Greater Than a Tourist book series, as well as the popular 50 Things to Know book series, we strive to help you learn about new places, spark your imagination, and inspire you. Wherever you are and whatever you do I wish you safe, fun, and inspiring travel.

Lisa Rusczyk Ed. D.
CZYK Publishing

>TOURIST

OUR STORY

Traveling is a passion of the "Greater than a Tourist" series creator. Lisa studied abroad in college, and for their honeymoon Lisa and her husband toured Europe. During her travels to Malta, an older man tried to give her some advice based on his own experience living on the island since he was a young boy. She was not sure if she should talk to the stranger but was interested in his advice. When traveling to some places she was wary to talk to locals because she was afraid that they weren't being genuine. Through her travels, Lisa learned how much locals had to share with tourists. Lisa created the "Greater Than a Tourist" book series to help connect people with locals. A topic that locals are very passionate about sharing.

>TOURIST

WELCOME TO
> TOURIST

>TOURIST

INTRODUCTION

Twenty years from now you will be more disappointed by the things you didn't do than by the ones you did. So throw off the bowlines, sail away from the safe harbor. Catch the trade winds in your sail. Explore. Dream. Discover. – Mark Twain

Adelaide is the smallest of the large cities in Australia, and as such, is often overlooked. This city manages to combine the best of the big city with the laid-back attitude that Australia is famous for.

Here, you can be in the middle of the city in the morning, and surrounded by wide open spaces without a hint of crowds before noon. The City of Churches offers something for everyone, and you're only limited by your imagination.

'Adelaide' isn't just Adelaide CBD. It's the entire region, from McLaren Vale to the Barossa, from the coast to the Adelaide Hills. It's part of the Aussie way of life.

>TOURIST

1. WHY VISIT ADELAIDE

Adelaide is the wine capital of Australia, with two of the largest wine regions within easy reach of the city. Adelaide and its surrounds are full of charming cafés and restaurants, absolutely bursting with cultural flavors. All of this is within a few hours' drive, leaving you with more time to enjoy it all.

Whether you're looking for beaches, wines, great food or walking trails, we have it all. The area is teeming with culture, both native and immigrant, and people are finding innovative ways of melding the two together, in art and in food.

With parks scattered throughout the city, you can breathe even as you enjoy the urban life, knowing that in 30 minutes you could be on a beach, sipping locally made wine as you chat with a new friend.

2. HOW TO GET AROUND

There are a number of ways you can get around Adelaide and the surrounding suburbs.

The main train station is on North Terrace, with lines extending north and south. From the train stops, if you're feeling adventurous, you can hop on a bus and see how far you can go.

Taxis and Uber are useful, but in my opinion, if you really want to be able to get around, renting a car is best. Trains and buses only run in the city and the outer suburbs, and there's so much more to Adelaide than that.

There are so many amazing places to see within two hour's drive of the city, so for your best experience, rent a car.

3. WHAT SIDE OF THE ROAD TO DRIVE ON

In Australia, we drive on the left side of the road. Our drivers sit on the right side of the car. So remember, the driver is closest to the center of the road.

If you have trouble with that, the police are pretty chill. They'll pull you over, but once you explain, they'll understand, though you may get a police driver and escort home. My dad did a couple times and there was never any trouble.

Also, slip lanes! Always use the slip lane for a left turn if it's there. If you miss it, your best bet is to go straight and turn around.

>TOURIST

4. PLACES TO STAY

Adelaide and the suburbs have the usual hotels, motels, and apartments to suit all tastes and budgets. If you're looking for something with a little more flavor, may I suggest Bed and Breakfasts?

The styles of B n B's are as varied as the people who run them, and many are in historical buildings. With a little extra looking, you could be staying in a quaint, adorable cottage with lovely country views, or in a picturesque home just a short walk from the beach.

For example:

Eagle Foundry Bed and Breakfast in historic Gawler was built around 1870, and during renovations they were very careful to restore the original look. It's an easy walk to Gawler's main street if you want to go out, but so comfortable inside that you may decide to stay put. My friend lives near Gawler and goes there for a weekend away.

Or, if you'd like a country setting, try The Cornishman's Cottage in One Tree Hill. Set in the original 170-year-old homestead on 12 acres of land, the farm is right on the edge of the Adelaide Hills. This is the perfect jump-off point for any country drives.

If you're looking for something close to the beach, Water Bay Villa Bed and Breakfast in Glenelg is a great choice. Just a 5-minute walk from the beach and 10 minutes' walk from Jetty Road, this 1910 house is perfectly situated for those looking for sun and sand. There's even a Heritage listed building right next door for added history.

5. PLACES TO SHOP

The most well-known place to shop in Adelaide is Rundle Mall. Located on Rundle Street, the entire road is closed to traffic and is pedestrian only. The street contains a huge range of stores, some of which are only available in Rundle Mall.

Central Market is one of the few markets around the world still within the city center. This market has fresh and artisan foods for all tastes. It's not unusual to have an entire meal picked up from various vendors within half an hour of entering.

If you're looking for outlet shopping, Harbor Town is your best option. Located just around the corner from the airport, Harbor Town has clothes, accessories, chocolates and a food court with views of

>TOURIST

the airport. Perfect, if you or your little ones like watching airplanes.

Jetty Road in Glenelg is just ten minutes down the road from Harbor Town. Containing high-end shops and ending in a jetty (hence the name), Jetty Road is brilliant for a day of shopping and sand.

6. GLENELG IS MORE THAN JETTY ROAD

When a person says Glenelg, most times all that's mentioned is Jetty Road, but two streets down there's Broadway. This is a quiet little street with cafés and restaurants, including an organic café and a restaurant that serves a limited gluten-free menu. A short walk away, the street ends at the ocean, and another café with views of the beach.

Fun fact: Glenelg is the site where European settlers first set foot in South Australia and is the oldest settlement there. The Old Gum Tree that SA was proclaimed a state under still stands, at 43 Mcfarlane St, Glenelg North.

7. PARKING AT GLENELG

If you're only going to Glenelg for a couple of hours, there's tons of 2-3 hour parking available just north of Jetty Road. However, if you're looking to make a day of it, you'll want something that doesn't require you to keep running around moving your car to avoid a fine.

There are roads running perpendicular to Jetty, between it and Pier Street, and between Pier and Broadway. It will take a bit more walking, maybe 10-15 minutes, but it's well worth it to avoid having to constantly remember to move your car. Look for road names like Morley, Partridge, and Penzance, though Partridge has a school on it. Between 8-9 am and 3-4 pm it gets very crowded as parents pick their kids up.

8. VISIT HENLEY BEACH

Henley Beach is slightly closer to the city than Glenelg and is great for a day on the beach. Most South Aussie beaches are dog-friendly, and Henley Beach is friendlier than most. You can usually see at least one dog gallivanting in the waves followed by its person.

>TOURIST

There are plenty of restaurants and cafés to suit all tastes. There's also a green with benches in sight of the ocean if you'd like to bring a picnic, so you'll have a hard time deciding where to eat. While you're there, why not stick around to watch the sunset?

There's plenty of free parking, and if you get there early, you can grab a space with unlimited time.

I should tell you, there's not much of what you'd call 'nightlife' at Henley. Maybe a couple of pubs or restaurants, but if you're looking for dancing and clubbing, we'll talk about that later.

9. SPEND A DAY AT SEMAPHORE

Semaphore's not just a beach (we're on a roll with beaches right now), it has tons of activities great for kids. In the warmer months, you have the Waterslide Complex, which includes mini golf, a jumping castle, and the Fort Glanville train rides. We always enjoy bringing the kids here during school holidays!

There's also the Foreshore Reserve, with a grassy space, covered playground, and a carousel. On the nearby Semaphore Road is where you'll find the ever-present cafes, shops, and restaurants.

Fun Fact: Semaphore has almost as long a history as Glenelg, particularly as a signal station. That was begun by a pub owner who was signaling his other pub in Port Adelaide!

10. PARKING GARAGES

If you're anywhere that's built up (such as Adelaide City Centre), you'll probably be parking in a garage. You can spend ages driving around, trying to find a vacancy or one that's tall enough to fit your car.

However, you can cut through all the hassle by booking a parking space online. It's quick and easy to book, and you can pick a specific parking garage. You can even specify how long you'll be there, and pay in advance.

I did this for my sister's birthday when we went to Adelaide for a couple of hours. There was a parade in town, and I wanted to make sure we had parking in a garage that was tall enough to fit our SUV. I had it done in less than 10 minutes and was able to get right back to party planning.

>TOURIST

11. SAY G'DAY, MATE

In the middle of all these beaches, you'll meet tons of locals. Believe it or not, most of them don't say 'g'day, mate.' That's more of an Outback thing.

We do tend to be a curious bunch, though, and love to get a conversation started.

Aussies are some of the most laid-back people I've ever met, and it carries over into conversations. They're prone to calling people 'luv.' If they do, no worries! 'Luv' is common, not a come on.

12. SUN SURVIVAL

The sun can be brutal in Australia, and Adelaide is no exception. Since we're upside down, our summer happens during the northern hemisphere's winter, which is an added shock to your system.

We have a saying here, for dealing with the sun: Slip, slap, slop, seek, and slide. Slip on a shirt, slap on a hat, slop on some sunscreen, seek shade and slide on some sunglasses. Follow this simple phrase and you shouldn't have to worry about burning.

Everybody, at one time or another, has sunburnt so badly that they've blistered. With 'slip, slap, slop, seek, and slide' we manage to avoid that. As a precaution, make sure to get some aloe vera gel when you buy your sunscreen. Aloe vera is the best way to soothe your skin and speed healing.

Try to drink at least three liters of water on warmer days, upping that number to five or six when the weather's hot. You lose far more water than you realize, so you need to stay hydrated.

13. ATTRACTIONS IN THE CITY

Adelaide is called the City of Churches, and the most famous of them is St Peter's Cathedral, located on King William Street between Adelaide and North Adelaide. St Peter's is open most days for free tours and is a great backdrop for photos.

If you're walking back to Adelaide, you'll cross over the River Torrens, and down on the banks in Elder Park, you'll see paddle boats. Those are available to rent, through Captain Jolleys Paddle Boats Elder Park. It's a lovely way to see the river, especially after a picnic in the park.

Test your wits at Escape Hunt Adelaide, right off Rundle Mall. Featuring three escape rooms with varying degrees of difficulty, they're awesome, and we crushed them all. Escape Hunt has a bar in the main room for you to celebrate your wins or drown your sorrows.

While you're on Rundle, check out the sculptures, like the pigs in the rubbish bin, or the giant Malls Balls (we love them, we just don't understand them).

Buskers dot the street, from musicians to magicians. If they're good, some folks will dance along, and the whole thing can turn into a mini-party.

The best time to check out performers on Rundle is the weekend, so head down there for a slow stroll. Don't miss out!

14. BEST PLACE FOR NIGHTLIFE

If you're looking for an evening out, with late night pubs, music, and dancing, your only true option is Hindley Street. From HQ, that has a separate room for each style of music, to The Wool Shed, that has country music and a mechanical bull, Hindley has got you covered.

If you're staying in the outer suburbs, and you want to drink, take the trains and Uber or make sure you have a designated driver. Cops will get you if you try drinking and driving. They're very fond of random breath tests and on the weekends you'll see them set up, pulling people over.

15. BUYING SOUVENIRS

Everybody wants that little memento of their trip, and in Australia, one of the most popular things to take home is a boomerang or ornament with Aboriginal painting on it. Thing is, most of those are made in China.

So if you're buying Aboriginal souvenirs, support our Indigenous people, and please make sure they're made by the Aboriginal peoples.

A great place to find them is at Tandanya National Aboriginal Culture Institute, which is an art gallery/museum located on Grenfell Street, on the edge of Adelaide CBD.

>TOURIST

16. CHECK OUT THE CHOCOLATE FACTORIES

If you're a fan of chocolate and want to see how it's made, we have two chocolate factories in the area.

Haigh's Chocolates in Adelaide not only has a retail shop but a factory where you can watch them making the different kinds of chocolates. Take a tour of the factory, then afterward, buy some of the chocolates you saw being made in their gift shop.

If you fancy a drive into the hills, Melba's Chocolate in Woodside is a great choice. They have a range of chocolates, from white to milk to dark, and candies in between. We go every time we head into the hills and it's our first stop before Hahndorf.

17. DRIVE THE ADELAIDE HILLS

Just an hour away from Adelaide city center you'll find yourself driving through the scenic Adelaide Hills. The towns feature unique shops and galleries with locally made wines and beers.

The most well-known of these amongst the South Aussies is Hahndorf. This German settlement has managed to stay true to its heritage through the years. The main street is chock full of pubs, cafes and gift shops stocked with local produce.

Start out walking down the main street, and by the time you get to the other end, your bags and bellies will be full. It's impossible to walk into Hahndorf and not see something to buy.

For art lovers, check out the Cedars, just a short drive from Hahndorf. The site where local artists Hans and Nora Heysen spent their lives and raised their family, you can walk the gardens and see where they drew inspiration for their artwork. There's a gallery, café and garden walk available.

From November to April, you can pick your own strawberries at Beerenberg Strawberry Farm, just outside of Hahndorf. Even if you decide not to go into the fields, their jams and preserves are available all year round. Try some with a local cheese, a bottle of wine, and enjoy the views from anywhere in the Hills.

The Farm Barn is perfect if you have little ones. It's a blend of a farmyard and wildlife park where kids can feed and pet the animals in supervised safety. During the Adelaide school holidays there are tons of extra activities for kids, too.

>TOURIST

18. THINGS TO WATCH OUT FOR WHILE DRIVING

When driving in the country, there are many things to be aware of. Kangaroos are most active in the morning and evening and can be very unpredictable. If you see one, slow down, more are nearby. They seem light and fluffy, but they can seriously damage a car. They're erratic in their movements, one minute hopping peacefully alongside the road, and the next they're trying to cut you off.

Koalas can occasionally be seen walking on the side of the road, and we honestly hope you'll be careful of our little cuties. They're rare enough as it is. Most places where they're seen have signs up warning you to be careful, so if you see one, keep your eye out for koalas.

The final thing to watch out for are cyclists. They're frequently seen on the roads, particularly the windy little ones. Most of those roads are narrow and very twisty, so places to safely pass them up are few and far between. Have patience with them!

19. WILDLIFE PARKS AND SANCTUARIES

For a closer look at native animals, there are a variety of wildlife parks and sanctuaries.

Humbug Scrub Wildlife Sanctuary is located north of Adelaide, on the edge of the Adelaide Hills, and is a not for profit run by locals that take in injured animals. Once the animal is healed, they're returned to the wild. If the animal is too injured to be released, then they have a forever home at the sanctuary.

Warrawong Wildlife Sanctuary is south of the city and recently re-opened in 2018 under new ownership. After being closed for many years, it's been given new life, so visit the sanctuary, have a coffee in the café, and enjoy nature!

The Big Rocking Horse in Gumeracha has a Wildlife Park available through the Toy Shop. The 7-acre park has both native and farm animals as well as an aviary. You can buy food in the store and take it through for the animals.

Gorge Wildlife Park in Cudlee Creek is located on 14 acres in the beautiful Adelaide Hills. This family owned park has a large collection of native animals that you can feed, and even a koala to hold. The animals also have a 'respite area' that they can go to if they're feeling overwhelmed. Perfect for children and families.

At Cleland Wildlife Park you can bring a picnic and spend the whole day with your family. Located just 20 minutes from Adelaide's city center, you'll be able to see the abrupt change between suburbs and gum forests. Cleland has many trails around, and they also offer night walks. The night skies in Australia are incredible, so why not go and enjoy the view?

20. PLACES TO DRINK

Listing places directly in Adelaide for food or drink would severely limit you. Some of the best wines I've had is in the outer suburbs and towns, like the Cellar Door, in Kersbrook.

Kersbrook Hills Wines and Ciders opened the Cellar Door in the old CFS building on the edge of the township. They have a range of ciders and wines, and are more than happy to walk you through a tasting to find something you like.

Uleybury Winery, just outside of One Tree Hill, is a family owned and run boutique winery. They also have a restaurant open on weekends that is amazing!

If you're looking to try a variety of drinks in one place, I'd have to suggest Bank Street Social on Hindley Street. It's worth it for the atmosphere alone, but they also specialize in South Australian boutique wines, craft beers, and gins. So if you feel you've only got one afternoon, this is the place to go.

21. PLACES TO EAT

The Topiary Cafe, in Tea Tree Gully is located in Newman's Nursery right on the edge of the hills. With food that is locally sourced, fresh, and often from within their own gardens, the Topiary is a gorgeous place to spend an afternoon. Even the drinks are made locally, so if you want to sample some of the best Adelaide has to offer, the Topiary is a great place to go.

Poetic Justice Café and Gallery is a hard one to fit into a single category. I have to include it here because the food is brilliant, but it goes beyond that. The café has only been open for three or four years, but they're already top 3 in Hospitality in Australia and top 10 for Customer Service Experience. Located in the northern town of Gawler, the café looks modest

>TOURIST

from the outside, but inside you'll soon be made to feel like an old friend.

I wandered in while my sister was getting a haircut about a year and a half ago. It was quiet, so I started chatting with Gayle, the owner. I got the gluten-free brownie, with homemade caramel sauce and a scoop of ice cream. I thought I died and went to heaven, and I don't usually like walnuts and sultanas (raisins) in my brownies.

They have a good range of both gluten-free and regular food, and most of their desserts are gluten-free. About 95% of the food is made in-house, and they keep everything as local as possible

Do you want a fruit smoothie? They have a list of fruits written on the board, and you can pick which ones you'd like mixed together. Interested in art? They have plenty from local artists hanging on the walls. My favorites are the Aboriginal style ones. The artist is of Aboriginal descent, so he takes a lot of inspiration from them, and both he and Gayle are very active within the community.

Simply Sushi in Glenelg is another must-try. It's a sushi train right on Jetty road, so you have the smell of the beach and the activity of one of our busiest streets right outside. Inside, you can sit down and relax with a cup of sake while picking and choosing from the train.

This was where I first tried raw tuna and I've never looked back. There are a few places I have to hit if I'm in Glenelg, and Simply Sushi is one of them.

I Love Crepes Café in Port Adelaide is another favorite of mine. I don't often find gluten-free products, but I Love Crepes has a whole range of sweet and savory crepes that can be done gluten free. Actually, the savories are only made GF. The owner says it's because the buckwheat batter is much stronger which allows him to begin adding the filling while the crepe is cooking. This gives the cheese time to melt and be all delicious.

This tiny shop on the corner of Commercial and St Vincent (the two main streets in Port Adelaide) features mostly al fresco seating, though there are a few tables and some bench seating inside. You'll quickly discover that Australia doesn't need strictly inside seating very often.

>TOURIST

22. SWEET CRAVINGS

Are you looking for something sweet after the drinking and the dining?

Bracegirdle's in Glenelg tops my list. They specialize in chocolate, from packages on the shelves to little chocolates in the glass-fronted case as well as a menu for those with time. Bracegirdle's is perfect for sitting on a chilly winter's day with a cup of one of their specialty hot chocolates and a book. This chocolate shop is an ideal place for a break during a day's exploration, or after playing on the beach.

Just Bliss Chocolates in Rundle Mall makes luxury chocolates that are absolutely beautiful as well as tasty. I particularly enjoy their alcoholic range, such as the gin and tonic filled chocolates and the Barossa Shiraz truffles. They also do house-made sweet or savory crepes. This ten-year-old company is family run, and you can even order online and they'll mail your chocolates to you.

Red Cacao in Stirling is unique because they don't mix chocolates from different regions. The chocolates in a single candy come from one region, what they call 'single origin'. You don't have to be a connoisseur to enjoy them, though you could use it as a chance to expand your knowledge.

Their chocolate café has a range of hot chocolates and specialty drinks. Coffee lovers can have a coffee matched with two chocolates. The staff is really knowledgeable, and great to talk to!

23. LOCAL CUISINE TO TRY

The Aboriginal peoples lived on nearly 6000 native plants, grains and meats, and there are some places where native food is featured.

Footeside Farm in Eudunda took their operation native during a drought. They decided to take their farming operation back to nature by planting natives, which require less water.

Footeside Farm is an innovator by planting and harvesting natives and having a food stand on their farm where you can stop and purchase fresh produce. Availability does depend on the time of year and what's in season.

Poetic Justice Café and Gallery roasts their own wattle seed and adds it to various dishes, such as damper and brownies. Soon, Gayle will be bringing out a cheese with wattle seed. Another native/contemporary combination that's a regular on the menu is lemon myrtle cake, which is very popular.

Kitchen Selva and Something Wild are located in Central Market. If you end up there, visit both! Something Wild specializes in meats and marinades, while Kitchen Selva has a few more plants to offer, as well as once a month dinners.

Central Market is an amazing way to find a variety of foods. Jagger cheese stand has a soft goat's cheese with saltbush. Saltbush is usually used as an alternative fodder for livestock. I hadn't been aware that it could be used for humans, too.

Kangaroo meat is a low-fat option that's very popular here, and available in many of the local shops, as well as restaurants. This is easily found in Central Market. Other things like emu, lemon myrtle, wattle seed, quandong and bush tomato are other natives available.

24. SHOULD YOU TIP

In short, no. While some countries have mandatory tipping, that's not the case in Adelaide. That being said, some places have a small tip jar near the till. If that's the case, definitely drop something in!

They usually save it for staff parties, with many employers taking their staff out for dinner and drinks around Christmas.

25. SHOPPING HOURS

This one's important. Shopping centers' hours are 9-5, except on late night shopping and Sundays. The northern and southern suburbs have late night shopping on Thursdays when they close at 9 pm. Adelaide's late night shopping is Friday, when they close at 9. On Sundays that time drops down to 11-4 or 5.

But wait! It gets worse. Grocery stores like Woolworths, Coles, Foodland, and Aldis are open from around 7, to 9 on weekdays. On the weekends, everything closes early, at 5 o'clock, though most still open at their weekday times.

Public Holidays here are actually holidays. Most stores close. It's really hit and miss which stores are open and which are closed. I still can't keep track. Shopping centers and grocery stores are all closed. With specialty stores it depends. If in doubt, consider it closed.

>TOURIST

26. VISIT THE BAROSSA VALLEY

With 80+ wineries in the Barossa Valley, you could spend your entire trip in the valley, going from one winery to another and never taste them all. Our preferred method for a tasting is to hire a bus or car company and take a tour for a day, that way we didn't have to worry about driving.

If you've done enough tasting, there's always helicopter rides with Adrenaline. My friend went and she said it was epic! The helicopter takes up to 3 people and you get a 30-minute tour of the Barossa.

Alternatively, if you want to stay a bit closer to the ground, Adrenaline also does horseback riding. I really liked the amount of time they take to make sure you're getting along with your horse, and that you're comfortable before you step onto the trail. We rode around the vineyard and the guide talked vines and wines.

There's plenty of accommodation in the Barossa, too. A few friends and I stayed at Novotel Barossa a couple of times, just for a weekend away. We were looking just to sit back and relax, and with so much onsite, we could've stayed put the whole weekend if we wanted. I did take advantage of the walking trails nearby.

While you're there, make your way to Tanunda, and give Beans and Cream a try. They have amazing gelato and sorbets. If you come in the summer, it's a must!

27. DRIVE TO MCLAREN VALE

Located south of the city, near the coast, the McLaren Vale wine region boasts 70+ wineries. Before you think that hitting one region is enough, don't forget that everything, from soil to the amount of sun, affects the flavor of wine. Down south there's a whole new bouquet to enjoy!

McLaren Vale is your stop if you're interested in a wine experience, but you still want beach time. Paddling the Onkaparinga River was my favorite thing to do down there. Enjoying the peace while floating down the river is an awesome experience.

If you want to see McLaren Vale from the air, fly in an open cockpit, Waco biplane with d'Arenburg. They also offer a range of experiences at their winery, such as blending and bottling your own wine.

>TOURIST

28. TAKE A DRIVE TO VICTOR HARBOR

About 2 hour's drive south of Adelaide, you can visit the town of Victor Harbor. Great for a few days away from the bustle of the city, Victor is relaxed and good if you have kids.

Granite Island is home to myriad animals, including penguins. You can get to the island by walking across the bridge, or wait to catch the horse-drawn tram. The horses are often stabled nearby, so the kids can get a close up look at the huge and gentle draft animals.

The penguins are our favourites and are really active at dawn and dusk. We always sat near the bridge in the evening with the sun setting at our backs to watch the penguins as they went about their evening routines. You can even get a guided tour around Granite Island to see the penguins.

There are boat tours to see more of the harbor, whale watching, both from the shore and by boat, as well as a Whale Centre. Whales are most active and closest to shore during the winter months, so from May to September. Remember, our seasons are backward!

Seeing as how this is South Australia, there's also wineries down there, locally made cheeses, and farms that actually allow you to U-pick. Last time I was there, I did a lot of cycling and walking. There are miles of paths, paved and clearly marked to make navigating them easier.

We never did the helicopter tours around Victor, though they are there. We just enjoyed the slower pace, watching the penguins and eating the fresh food.

29. SEE PORT ADELAIDE

Home to one of South Australia's two AFL teams, Port Power, Port Adelaide is a historic city, being one of the major ports for this state. The historic old town is the best, and most scenic part of the town.

Start by taking a tour of a historic treasure, The City of Adelaide. This clipper ship was built in 1864 specifically to transport citizens from the UK and Europe to Adelaide. Now, she sits out of the water undergoing preservation and some restoration work so that many more people can see her in the coming years.

>TOURIST

A little farther down the waterfront, there's a tugboat that offers rides. You can easily book those through the Maritime Museum. The Dolphin Explorer also docks here, if you're looking for a tour with a purpose.

Several great museums live in Port Adelaide, like the Maritime Museum, the Railway Museum, and the Aviation Museum. Then there's the food! The I Love Crepes Café is a short walk from the docks, and there's a variety of pubs with local brews and wines available. There's a pizza place, El Greco, that does brilliant specialty pizzas, and all of them can be done gluten free.

If you're into arts, there are little galleries of local artists that dot the streets, though their openings are usually advertised via posters around the city.

If you're walking down St Vincent, check out True Hemp Culture, which features clothing made with hemp and bamboo. They're tougher, last longer, and have anti-bacterial properties. Boutique clothing, toy, and antique stores line the streets around it.

On Sundays only, there's the Fisherman's Wharf Market, which is much larger and more eclectic than I was expecting. There's the usual round of knick-knacks that grandma loves, jewelry, books, and movies. They also have an entire stall dedicated to bicycles, and more to collectibles, and antiques. While you may not buy, it's a fun way to spend a bit of free time while you're waiting for your boat ride. There are coffee and pastry stands available, too.

30. SEE THE BOTANIC GARDENS

The Adelaide Botanic Gardens are a popular haunt for us, especially those looking for beautiful scenery for photos. The Botanic Gardens are a popular place for professional photos. My sister got her wedding photos done here.

These aren't just beautiful paths through cultivated plants, though. The Gardens run free guided walks to teach you more about the plants, and they have exotics like orchids as well as natives for us all to learn about.

Best of all are the activities. Half the time, if you're going to a concert, you're heading to the Botanic Gardens. Plays and concerts are side by side with classes on botany, and how to take cuttings. We go to learn more about plants, cuttings, seedlings, soil, and compost, but the Garden offers so much for all types.

>TOURIST

During most summers the Gardens hosts outdoor movie screenings. All you have to do is bring the chairs and popcorn. They also have exhibitions all year round, on topics from glass blowing to textiles.

They even have sister gardens in Mount Lofty and Wittunga, if you're feeling like a wander. Each has something different to offer. Wittunga is great because it's a haven for wildlife so if you're hoping to see birds, butterflies and the like, it's perfect. Mount Lofty has amazing walking trails, as well as a lake and sculptures.

31. MORIALTA CONSERVATION AND RECREATION PARK

If you're looking for waterfalls, this is the place to go. We don't get to see them too often, so Morialta is where we head when we feel like seeing fresh water falling down a cliff. There's a range of walking trails around the park, most of which are moderate to difficult. You can go any time of year, but for the best waterfalls, winter to spring is best. There's also more wildflowers blooming at those times.

Morialta is great for kids because there's an adventure park that's perfect for older children.

Recently finished, the playground has a 7-meter tall nest that looks incredible. The entire theme of the playground is nature, with most of the playsets being made out of wood, and left as natural as possible.

For the adventurous and experienced, there's rock climbing and abseiling points further in the park, as well as trails for mountain biking. If you're walking, keep an eye on the signs. Near the rock climbing and abseiling points, there will be warnings to turn back.

32. THE BEST WALKING TRAILS AROUND ADELAIDE

If you're looking for more places to get out and about and explore nature, there are a number of beautiful walks around the city. Mt Lofty is one of the most popular in my family.

Don't expect huge peaks and massive mountain ranges. Australia is one of the most weathered continents and our mountains in SA are fairly well ground down. What this means is that you can actually walk to the top and enjoy the scenery the whole way.

Mt Lofty has a number of walks around it, with my favorite being the one from Waterfall Gully to the

>TOURIST

Mt Lofty Summit. It's classed as a more difficult hike, and there are sections of the trail that can be quite steep. There's cafés and parking at either end, though if you park at the summit you'll have to face the steep uphill on the way back. It's about 3 hours return trip, and I'd recommend this for active people.

The River Torrens Linear Trail is a 21.7 mile trek from West Beach, through Adelaide CBD to Athelstone at the edge of the Adelaide Hills. This trail is accessible from a number of parking lots and is even wheelchair accessible.

The River Torrens trail is a verdant haven in the midst of the city, surrounded by red gums and reed beds with plenty of parks, parking, and toilets along the way. All you need to find it is the name and Google Maps.

Depending on where you decide to walk, there may be occasional major road crossings, though the builders put bridges and underpasses where possible. In the summertime, there won't be much surface water. However, the underground water shows in the varied plant life, so there's plenty to look at.

My last specific recommendation is the Waterfall Hike at Belair National Park. Another lovely bushwalk in the Adelaide Hills, this one should take you about 3 hours and is considered moderate. This path is actually a loop, unlike the other two, and sometimes it follows fire tracks that are shared with cyclists. So if you end up walking on a wider, gravel path, no worries, mate.

You're not likely to see any water flowing unless you're up after a heavy rain, but if you keep your eyes open, you've got a great chance of seeing local wildlife. Keep a watch on birds in particular, because there's some gorgeous color flying around out there. If you hear one that sounds like crazy laughter, you're listening to a kookaburra, everyone's favorite.

Before going on any walks, make sure you're following sun precautions, bring plenty of water and something to deal with the mosquitoes. Your walk will be much more enjoyable if you prepare for it.

33. LOCAL FISHING CHARTERS

Most fishing charter's storefronts are located a bit farther inland, so it's advisable to find and book them online.

Get Hooked Fishing Charter is located on Anzac Highway, just south of the city. They have a 5-star rating that's well deserved. You can get the full day or half day charters, though we always prefer to go out for a full day. Get Hooked has got all the latest gadgets and safety gear, plus plenty of know-how to find the fishes.

They also have tailored tours for up to 3 days, but I've never tried one of those. I don't have sea legs, so one day on a boat is about all my stomach can stand.

Strike 1 Fishing Charter is another top-notch charter company. Albert is brilliant, and they have a range of tour options to choose from. You can even go for tuna, with 9 hours allocated to catch one. A bit of browsing shows that Albert and Strike 1 are intent on making sure everybody has an awesome day, with them going above and beyond. It's always good to know it's happened more than once.

34. TOP FISHING SPOTS

Any local who enjoys fishing will tell you that the top spots are a bit of a drive away. We personally prefer making the 8-hour drive to the Eyre Peninsula, camping at Elliston, and driving to fishing spots from there. Our favorite beach in that area is Locks Wells. We go during Christmas week for an entire week of surf fishing. At the beginning of the week you're catching whiting, and at the end, you're catching salmon.

There's also Ceduna, where you can surf fish or get a charter boat, Scotts Bay, which is one of the best salmon fishing points anywhere, and Cowell, that has a harbor and a wide variety of fish. There's no end to the places you could go on the Eyre Peninsula. This is an 8-hour drive, though, and we'd be gone for a week or two.

So if that's too far, next on the list is the Yorke Peninsula. Literally, every place I could possibly think to name has great fishing, or crabbing, or, well, anything seafood.

The best part about the Yorke Peninsula is that it's all 2-4 hours away from Adelaide. You could easily do an overnight stay and get some solid fishing hours in between.

For example, Edithburgh is only 3 hours away from Adelaide and, depending on the season, you can find squid, salmon, flathead, snook, and Tommy Ruffs. Most of Adelaide's major fishing is done from the Yorke Peninsula.

Finally, if you'd rather keep it completely local, you can drop a line from a jetty. The Brighton, Glenelg, Henley Beach and Semaphore jetties are about 30 minutes from Adelaide, so if all you want to do is drop a line and watch the horizon, these places are brilliant.

35. BEST BEACHES FOR SURFING

Kangaroo Island, with the best beaches to surf on in the Adelaide area, is a few hours' drive and a ferry ticket away. All told, it comes to about 4 hours. From what I hear from my friends, Kangaroo Island is mostly for more advanced surfers, so you should make sure you have an adequate skill level.

If you choose KI, you will need to make sure you've rented a 4 wheel drive, as the tracks there can get rough. Vivonne Bay is my friends' favorite, as it suits all levels.

The Fleurieu Peninsula, where the ferry for Kangaroo Island is located, has awesome surfing beaches. Fleurieu is an easy drive south from Adelaide. There are a number of beaches such as Moana, Christies Beach, Southport and Sellicks Beach that are suitable for all levels.

One you have to watch out for is Waitpinga. There are riptides out there, and an inexperienced surfer or one unfamiliar with the beach should avoid it. That won't be hard to do, as Fleurieu has so much else to offer.

36. BEST BEACHES FOR SNORKELLING AND DIVING

About 45 minutes south of Adelaide, you have Port Noarlunga, and the Port Noarlunga Reef. The reef is just a few hundred meters offshore, and easily accessible to both snorkelers and divers.

Continuing south from there is Rapid Bay and Second Valley. They and Port Noarlunga are part of the Encounter Marine Park, which is a fairly long stretch, taking nearly an hour to drive, depending on the traffic. All 3 of these places have a wide variety of marine life, and I could spend all day in the water and never get tired. There's even another reef at Second Valley.

You can dive a shipwreck off Fleurieu Peninsula, at Marina St Vincent. You'll have to take a boat to reach it, though.

I would be remiss if I didn't mention the two Maritime Heritage Trails off the Yorke Peninsula. I've never been, but I got to chatting with a gentleman who's been diving since he was a young man, and he

>TOURIST

highly recommends them. They are the Wardang Island Maritime Heritage Trail and the Investigator Strait Shipwreck Trail. What makes these so awesome is the ten shipwrecks located along the two trails.

The water off the Yorke Peninsula is incredibly clear, and there are great snorkeling spots all along the way. You could even see seahorses at Edithburgh jetty (where there's also amazing fishing!).

37. BEST PLACES TO RENT UNDERWATER GEAR

When it comes to renting gear or taking classes, we only go with PADI companies. Their reputation is the best, and they can be found all over the world, so no matter where you are, you can be sure of a fun, safe outing with professional, well-trained divers.

In Adelaide, there are a few PADI places. Diving Adelaide, just to the south of Adelaide CBD, on South Road, offers both rentals and courses for the new. They will take you to a variety of places, including Edithburgh jetty, so if you'd like a professional along, try Diving Adelaide.

Adelaide Scuba in Glenelg also offers PADI courses and gear rental. They're also extremely familiar with Glenelg, having operated there for years. You can get tours and 3-day intensive courses in diving. Adelaide Scuba, in conjunction with Glenelg Scuba Diving Club, actually look after many of the dive sites in the area.

For a PADI dive shop north of the city, check out Underwater Sports Diving Centre. With a wide range of courses, if you're just starting to either leveling up, Underwater Sports can help you.

Really, the major differences between them are availability, pricing, and locations for tours. As I said earlier, as long as they're PADI certified, you know you're in good hands.

38. THE BEST WAY TO SEE DOLPHINS

To see dolphins, you can either head to a beach or take a dolphin tour to see these playful creatures.

There's the Adelaide Dolphin Sanctuary, located on Port River, near Port Adelaide. They've got about 40 dolphins who live there, with another 300 who come and go. You can walk the self-guided Port

>TOURIST

River Dolphin Trail, or rent a kayak and go on the river. I've always gone kayaking along the river, and more often than not, we'll see a few dolphins playing around us.

Freeman's Knob, on Fleurieu Peninsula, is very popular with a pod of dolphins and offers great lookout points at Encounter Bay and Horseshoe Bay. This one's good if you're not wanting to move too much, or traveling with the elderly or children.

You can go on boat tours to see dolphins as well. Port Adelaide has several charters to choose from, such as the Dolphin Explorer Cruises located right on the wharf, at Berth 2. Or you could try a smaller, more interesting, boat, and go with the South Australian Maritime Museum Heritage Boats.

Further south, there is Dolphin Boat, where you may have the opportunity to swim with dolphins. You can't do this on your own in the wild, for the dolphin's wellbeing and safety, but Dolphin Boat's Temptation is one of the few boats that's been given a license to offer these tours.

39. SAFETY AT THE BEACH

Australia is home to blue-green waters and golden sand beaches, so it's easy to think they're all perfect, but for the best experience, there are a few precautions you need to know.

Many beaches that are normally safe can, under the wrong circumstances such as high winds, become dangerous. Surf Life Saving SA (SLSA) suggests only swimming on patrolled beaches, between the red and yellow flags and never swimming alone.

For the most up to date information about beach facilities, patrol status, weather, swells, and tide, download the Beachsafe App.

40. THE BEST FESTIVALS

The biggest festival here is the Adelaide Fringe, which shows up every February and lasts an entire month. The Fringe feels like it takes up the entire city while it runs, and it actually does, with over 1200 acts. There is a huge variety to the acts, so there's seriously something for everyone. When the Fringe is in town, life is wild and free. If you could only come here once, come during the Fringe.

WOMADelaide is a much smaller, open-air festival in Adelaide's Botanic Park. Usually beginning near the end of the Fringe, WOMADelaide lasts 4 days and has contemporary and traditional music, arts, dancing, and food. Like all the best things, it has to be experienced at least once in your life.

For a bit of variety, there's Tasting Australia, 10 days of food and wine held in April. Adelaide is the wine center of Australia and is on the fast track for being a foodie's paradise, so if you're into good eats and great drinks, this is your festival. It's the best way to taste everything the region has to offer without racking up the mileage on your car.

41. MUST SEE MUSEUMS

The South Australian Museum on North Terrace is one I've been to several times. There are natural history and scientific research exhibits, but what they're truly well-known for is their Aboriginal studies and displays. Sadly, the native memory was nearly wiped out, but now initiatives are being taken to properly educate folks about Aboriginal cultures and heritage.

If you want a more in-depth look at the various cultures that make up today's melting pot of people, the Migration Museum is for you. They trace Aboriginal culture pre-colonisation and even the impact and history of settlement. Much smaller than the South Australian Museum, and only a short walk away from it, the Migration Museum is located on Kintore St, just off North Terrace.

Tandanya National Aboriginal Cultural Institute focuses on Aboriginal and Torres Strait Islander culture and art. They have performances as well as paintings and visual artwork available. If you're looking for genuine artwork to take home, this is a great place to go. Parking for Tandanya would be the most difficult, so it's a good idea to check out the tips about parking garages before you go.

42. THE BEST TIME TO VISIT

This varies, depending on what you're interested in. Personally, autumn and spring are my favorite times. There are still plenty of warm days to enjoy the beach without the insanely hot weather that comes with summer. The beaches also tend to be a little less

>TOURIST

crowded. It's mostly dry, so there's nothing to rain on your parade.

If you come in summer, be aware that you'll need to take lots of sun precautions. The temperature can get up to 113* F for several days in a row, and you don't realize how bad it is until you're in it.

Winters are mild and we never see snow around Adelaide, though on occasion it can get chilly. You're better off bringing your own winter clothes rather than buying them here, if you decide to come between June and September.

43. HOW TO USE ROUNDABOUTS

Roundabouts are a fact of driving in Australia, and Adelaide has more than its fair share. If you don't want to cause a pile-up, there are a few things you should know.

First off, NEVER stop in a roundabout. Those other cars waiting to get in can take care of themselves. Your job is to get through quickly and efficiently so the other drivers can get moving.

As you approach a roundabout, slow down and look to your right (remember, we drive on the left). If there are no cars, or there is a gap big enough to fit you, go. Otherwise, it's okay to wait

Signaling is important! If you're turning left, signal like normal. If you're going straight, don't signal until you're exiting, to let the other driver know you're leaving. If you're turning right, signal right until you get to the exit you want, then signal left. This applies if you're in a roundabout with 4 or more exits.

Finally, watch the other drivers and cars. Most folks take signaling very seriously, and it's rare to see someone not using their turn signals. When in doubt, wait. Ignore the guy behind you.

44. BASIC BUSHWALKING SAFETY TIPS

Snakes are a part of life here, and its best you're prepared and aware. Brown snakes are really the only ones you have to worry about, and in 16 years in South Australia, I've seen one maybe 4 times, so it's not a big deal. Still, basic safety tips are important and are why I don't know anyone who's ever been bitten by a snake.

>TOURIST

Anytime you're walking in the bush, make noise. The snakes will hear you and get out of your way. Believe it or not, they're quite shy, and not aggressive as long as you don't actively look for them.

Stick to the trails. Snakes will be in little corners that you're not expecting, and these guys don't have warning systems.

If you see an injured animal, like a kangaroo or koala, do not approach. They can be dangerous when frightened. Instead, make note of where the animal is and contact the rangers. Most parks have contact numbers at the entrance, so take a photo of that before you head in. They'll send a ranger in to help the injured animal as soon as possible.

If you see a lizard with a wedge-shaped head and matching tail, that maybe has a blue tongue, you just met your new best friend. Those guys are blue-tongued skinks, and they eat snakes. We always see a few around at my mom's house in the hills, and we rarely see snakes.

45. SPIDER SAFETY TIPS

If you're staying in metropolitan centers like Adelaide, spiders aren't really an issue, but if you're planning to head out, you should be aware of a few things.

Those little spiders with the longs legs and not much body to speak of? Those are daddy long legs and not a problem. They make webs, stay up high, and don't have fangs long enough to make it through human skin. They're harmless.

That tarantula looking guy, with the narrow abdomen and upper legs that spread out like the facehuggers in Alien? He's good. In fact, he's great! That's a huntsman, and they're the good guys. They look scary, but they eat the bugs that attract the really harmful spiders. Just make sure you know where they're at and they can't surprise you.

However, there's another tarantula, with a larger body, shorter legs, and looks more like your classic tarantula, who you only see in spring. That guy is a trapdoor spider and is dangerous. Don't let them close. If you're able, vacuum them up. If not, tell staff or an Aussie about the little guy.

The other one that's on my immediate hit list is much smaller, grey with a long, slender abdomen that

>TOURIST

has a white patch on the tip of it. That one is called a white tip and should be killed right away. They are highly venomous, but that's where the huntsman comes in. Huntsmen eat the same bugs white tips like, thus keeping white tips out of your space. If you're not comfortable dealing with a spider, do please tell the staff.

Lastly, we have the redback. They're similar to black widows, except that the red mark is on the back. They usually lurk in dark, out of the way places, so they're not often seen.

You're not likely to see these spiders, but again, having the basic knowledge is useful. I don't know anyone who's ever been bitten by a spider, and just being aware that these guys are here really helps with safety.

46. CONSERVE THE WATER

South Australia is the driest state in the driest continent in the world. As a result, we take water conservation very seriously here.

One thing is that all toilets have two options for flushing. One of them uses only half a tank, and we ask that you use that option as often as possible.

Another thing is to turn off hoses and taps between uses (I know, nine times out of ten, none of this will be an issue for you, but bear with me here). Keep showers to a minimum as much as possible. If you have a leaky tap, let maintenance, the front desk or your landlord know as quickly as possible.

47. REMEMBER TO STAY HYDRATED

Things are very dry here, so it's important to drink plenty of water. The recommended amount is 3 liters a day minimum. On a hot day, especially if you're active, 4-6 liters is necessary.

Make sure you're getting plenty of electrolytes. You can either pick up an energy drink at the shops, or some electrolyte tablets from the shops or chemists. Rule of thumb with a sports drink is to keep drinking it until it doesn't taste good anymore. That's how you know you've finally replenished your electrolytes.

If you feel slightly dizzy, stop what you're doing, find some shade and get some water. Heat stress is a less intense form of heat stroke, but it can still take a while to fully recover.

>TOURIST

Make sure the people around you are also drinking enough. On hot days, the radio will send out warnings advising people to avoid alcohol, as that will dehydrate you. If you do choose to drink just make sure you're in a cool environment first.

48. DEALING WITH MOSQUITOES

Mosquitoes come out in droves in the evenings. And mornings. And any time of day that is comfortable for them. Basically, the only time you won't see them is in winter.

Mosquitoes (aka mozzies) are tiny, numerous, and surprisingly loud. However, they have one weakness: citronella. You can buy citronella candles, tiki torches, and sprays. The sprays are more effective than Deet (the popular chemical brand) and kinder on your body.

Deet is an insect repellent, but it's full of chemicals, and if you're sensitive or have allergies, it's best to avoid it. I find that the citronella options are more effective while smelling nice.

If you do get bites, there are a number of anti-itch sprays, but we prefer Stingos. It takes the itch off right away and reduces the swelling, though it does leave a white mark. Just make sure you clean it off before you go out.

We've also found taking vitamin B makes you less attractive to mozzies. You get bitten less often and the bites don't itch as much.

49. COMMON COLLOQUIALISMS

Aussies have a number of slang words that go beyond 'fair dinkum' and 'g'day, mate.' Understanding them will make life and conversation much easier, especially since Aussies can be a friendly, chatty bunch.

For a start, if you're giving someone the peace sign, there's something you should know. Always have your palm facing the other person. Never show them the back of your hand when you've got your index and middle fingers up. That's more like giving someone the middle finger times two.

Another colloquialism you just got introduced to above. Mozzie is short for mosquito. Here's a few more:

Jumper = sweatshirt

>TOURIST

No worries = no problem - sure thing - okay - yeah

Cheers = thanks for that - thanks for the drink - hey, I've got a drink!

Servo = gas station - petrol station

Tap = faucet

She's all right = it's all good - everything's fine

Sunnies = Sunglasses

Arvo = Afternoon

The suffix 'zzie' or 'zza' = a lot of words and names are shortened by adding those suffixes. 'Daryl' turns into 'Dazza,' or 'mosquito' turns into 'mozzie.' When Aussies start talking fast, these suffixes get flung around a lot, and knowing they exist makes talking with them much easier.

Basically, Aussies will shorten any word they can. Just ask them to slow down and maybe explain a little, though if they're in a group, good luck.

50. 'NO SHOES, NO SHIRT, NO SERVICE,' NOT EXACTLY

There are a number of places where it's perfectly acceptable to walk around shirtless or shoeless. If you're at the beach, and you want to sit in a café or restaurant on the foreshore, most places have no problem with you wandering in wearing shorts or a cover-up. If you're unsure, the establishment will usually have a sign outside, or you can catch the attention of an employee to check and make sure.

I've seen people going to the store real quick barefoot, or into the petrol station to pay for petrol without shoes and no one looks twice. In a country where the standard wear is shorts, tank top, and flip-flops, we don't stand on ceremony very much.

>TOURIST

TOP REASONS TO BOOK THIS TRIP

Beaches: The beaches here are the best.

Wine: We have so many different, excellent wines. There's something for everyone.

Lifestyle: Adelaide is relaxed and laid back

\>TOURIST

BONUS BOOK

50 THINGS TO KNOW ABOUT PACKING LIGHT FOR TRAVEL

PACK THE RIGHT WAY EVERY TIME

AUTHOR: MANIDIPA BHATTACHARYYA

First Published in 2015 by Dr. Lisa Rusczyk. Copyright 2015. All Rights Reserved. No part of this publication may be reproduced, including scanning and photocopying, or distributed in any form or by any means, electronic or mechanical, or stored in a database or retrieval system without prior written permission from the publisher.

Disclaimer: The publisher has put forth an effort in preparing and arranging this book. The information provided herein by the author is provided "as is". Use this information at your own risk. The publisher is not a licensed doctor. Consult your doctor before engaging in any medical activities. The publisher and author disclaim any liabilities for any loss of profit or commercial or personal damages resulting from the information contained in this book.

Edited by Melanie Howthorne

ABOUT THE AUTHOR

Manidipa Bhattacharyya is a creative writer and editor, with an education in English literature and Linguistics. After working in the IT industry for seven long years she decided to call it quits and follow her heart instead. Manidipa has been ghost writing, editing, proof reading and doing secondary research services for many story tellers and article writers for about three years. She stays in Kolkata, India with her husband and a busy two year old. In her own time Manidipa enjoys travelling, photography and writing flash fiction.

Manidipa believes in travelling light and never carries anything that she couldn't haul herself on a trip. However, travelling with her child changed the scenario. She seemed to carry the entire world with her for the baby on the first two trips. But good sense prevailed and she is again working her way to becoming a light traveler, this time with a kid.

INTRODUCTION

He who would travel happily must travel light.

-Antoine de Saint-Exupéry

Travel takes you to different places from seas and mountains to deserts and much more. In your travels you get to interact with different people and their cultures. You will, however, enjoy the sights and interact positively with these new people even more, if you are travelling light.

When you travel light your mind can be free from worry about your belongings. You do not have to spend precious vacation time waiting for your luggage to arrive after a long flight. There is be no chance of your bags going missing and the best part is that you need not pay a fee for checked baggage.

People who have mastered this art of packing light will root for you to take only one carry-on, wherever you go. However, many people can find it really hard to pack light. More so if you are travelling with children. Differentiating between "must have" and "just in case" items is the starting point. There will be ample shopping avenues at your destination which are just waiting to be explored.

This book will show you 'packing' in a new 'light' – pun intended – and help you to embrace light packing practices for all of your future travels.

Off to packing!

DEDICATION

I dedicate this book to all the travel buffs that I know, who have given me great insights into the contents of their backpacks.

THE RIGHT TRAVEL GEAR

1. CHOOSE YOUR TRAVEL GEAR CAREFULLY

While selecting your travel gear, pick items that are light weight, durable and most importantly, easy to carry. There are cases with wheels so you can drag them along – these are usually on the heavy side because of the trolley. Alternatively a backpack that you can carry comfortably on your back, or even a duffel bag that you can carry easily by hand or sling across your body are also great options. Whatever you choose, one thing to keep in mind is that the luggage itself should not weigh a ton, this will give you the flexibility to bring along one extra pair of shoes if you so desire.

\>TOURIST

2. CARRY THE MINIMUM NUMBER OF BAGS

Selecting light weight luggage is not everything. You need to restrict the number of bags you carry as well. One carry-on size bag is ideal for light travel. Most carriers allow one cabin baggage plus one purse, handbag or camera bag as long as it slides under the seat in front. So technically, you can carry two items of luggage without checking them in.

3. PACK ONE EXTRA BAG

Always pack one extra empty bag along with your essential items. This could be a very light weight duffel bag or even a sturdy tote bag which takes up minimal space. In the event that you end up buying a lot of souvenirs, you already have a handy bag to stuff all that into and do not have to spend time hunting for an appropriate bag.

> *I'm very strict with my packing and have everything in its right place. I never change a rule. I hardly use anything in the hotel room. I wheel my own wardrobe in and that's it.*
>
> Charlie Watts

CLOTHES & ACCESSORIES

4. PLAN AHEAD

Figure out in advance what you plan to do on your trip. That will help you to pick that one dress you need for the occasion. If you are going to attend a wedding then you have to carry formal wear. If not, you can ditch the gown for something lighter that will be comfortable during long walks or on the beach.

5. WEAR THAT JACKET

Remember that wearing items will not add extra luggage for your air travel. So wear that bulky jacket that you plan to carry for your trip. This saves space and can also help keep you warm during the chilly flight.

6. MIX AND MATCH

Carry clothes that can be interchangeably used to reinvent your look. Find one top that goes well with a couple of pairs of pants or skirts. Use tops, shirts and jackets wisely along with other accessories like a scarf or a stole to create a new look.

>TOURIST

7. CHOOSE YOUR FABRIC WISELY

Stuffing clothes in cramped bags definitely takes its toll which results in wrinkles. It is best to carry wrinkle free, synthetic clothes or merino tops. This will eliminate the need for that small iron you usually bring along.

8. DITCH CLOTHES PACK UNDERWEAR

Pack more underwear and socks. These are the things that will give you a fresh feel even if you do not get a chance to wear fresh clothes. Moreover these are easy to wash and can be dried inside the hotel room itself.

9. CHOOSE DARK OVER LIGHT

While picking your clothes choose dark coloured ones. They are easy to colour coordinate and can last longer before needing a wash. Accidental food spills and dirt from the road are less visible on darker clothes.

10. WEAR YOUR JEANS

Take only one pair of Jeans with you, which you should wear on the flight. Remember to pick a pair that can be worn for sightseeing trips and is equally eloquent for dinner. You can add variety by adding light weight cargoes and chinos.

11. CARRY SMART ACCESSORIES

The right accessory can give you a fresh look even with the same old dress. An intelligent neck-piece, a couple of bright scarves, stoles or a sarong can be used in a number of ways to add variety to your clothing. These light weight beauties can double up as a nursing cover, a light blanket, beach wear, a modesty cover for visiting places of worship, and also makes for an enthralling game of peek-a-boo.

12. LEARN TO FOLD YOUR GARMENTS

Seasoned travellers all swear by rolling their clothes for compact and wrinkle free packing. Bundle packing, where you roll the clothes around a central object as if tying it up, is also a popular method of compact and wrinkle free packing. Stacking folded clothes one on top of another is a big no-no as it makes creases extreme and they are difficult to get rid of without ironing.

>TOURIST

13. WASH YOUR DIRTY LAUNDRY

One of the ways to avoid carrying loads of clothes is to wash the clothes you carry. At some places you might get to use the laundry services or a Laundromat but if you are in a pinch, best solution is to wash them yourself. If that is the plan then carrying quick drying clothes is highly recommended, which most often also happen to be the wrinkle free variety.

14. LEAVE THOSE TOWELS BEHIND

Regular towels take up a lot of space, are heavy and take ages to dry out. If you are staying at hotels they will provide you with towels anyway. If you are travelling to a remote place, where the availability of towels look doubtful, carry a light weight travel towel of viscose material to do the job.

15. USE A COMPRESSION BAG

Compression bags are getting lots of recommendation now days from regular travellers. These are useful for saving space in your luggage when you have to pack bulky dresses. While packing for the return trip, get help from the hotel staff to arrange a vacuum cleaner.

FOOTWEAR

16. PUT ON YOUR HIKING BOOTS

If you have plans to go hiking or trekking during your trip, you will need those bulky hiking boots. The best way to carry them is to wear them on flight to save space and luggage weight. You can remove the boots once inside and be comfortable in your socks.

17. PICKING THE RIGHT SHOES

Shoes are often the bulkiest items, along with being the dainty if you are a female. They need care and take up a lot of space in your luggage. It is advisable therefore to pick shoes very carefully. If you plan to do a lot of walking and site seeing, then wearing a pair of comfortable walking shoes are a must. For more formal occasions you can carry durable, light weight flats which will not take up much space.

18. STUFF SHOES

If you happen to pack a pair of shoes, ensure you utilize their hollow insides. Tuck small items like rolled up socks or belts to save space. They will also be easy to find.

> TOURIST

TOILETRIES

19. STASHING TOILETRIES

Carry only absolute necessities. Airline rules dictate that for one carry-on bag, liquids and gels must be in 3.4 ounce (100ml) bottles or less, and must be packed in a one quart zip-lock bag. If you are planning to stay in a hotel, the basic things will be provided for you. It's best is to buy the rest from the local market at your destination.

20. TAKE ALONG TAMPONS

Tampons are a hard to find item in a lot of countries. Figure out how many you need and pack accordingly. For longer stays you can buy them online and have them delivered to where you are staying.

21. GET PAMPERED BEFORE YOU TRAVEL

Some avid travellers suggest getting a pedicure and manicure just the day before travelling. This not only gives you a well kept look, you also save the trouble of packing nail polish. Remember, every little bit of weight reduced adds up.

ELECTRONICS

22. LUGGING ALONG ELECTRONICS

Electronics have a large role to play in our lives today. Most of us cannot imagine our lives away from our phones, laptops or tablets. However while travelling, one must consider the amount of weight these electronics add to our luggage. Thankfully smart phones come along with all the essentials tools like a camera, email access, picture editing tools and more. They are smart to the point of eliminating the need to carry multiple gadgets. Choose a smart phone that suits all your requirements and travel with the world in your palms or pocket.

23. REDUCE THE NUMBER OF CHARGERS

If you do travel with multiple electronic devices, you will have to bear the additional burden of carrying all their chargers too. Check if a single charger can be used for multiple devices. You might also consider investing in a pocket charger. These small devices support multiple devices while keeping you charged on the go.

>TOURIST

24. TRAVEL FRIENDLY APPS

Along with smart phones come numerous apps, which are immensely helpful in our travels. You name it and you have an app for it at hand – take pictures, sharing with friends and family, torch to light dark roads, maps, checking flight/train times, find hotels and many other things. Use these smart alternatives to traditional items like books to eliminate weight and save space.

I get ideas about what's essential when packing my suitcase.

-Diane von Furstenberg

TRAVELLING WITH KIDS

25. BRING ALONG THE STROLLER

Kids might enjoy walking for a while but they soon tire out and a stroller is the just the right thing for them to rest in while you continue your tour. Strollers also double duty as a luggage carrier and shopping bag holder. Remember to pick a light weight, easy to handle brand of stroller. Better yet, find out in advance if you can rent a stroller at your destination.

26. BRING ONLY ENOUGH DIAPERS FOR YOUR TRIP

Diapers take up a lot of space and add to the weight of your luggage. Therefore it is advisable to carry just enough diapers to last through the trip and a few for afterwards, till you buy fresh stock at your destination. Unless of course you are travelling to a really remote area, in which case you have no choice but to carry the load. Otherwise diapers are something you will find pretty easily.

27. TAKE ONLY A COUPLE OF TOYS

Children are easily attracted by new things in their environment. While travelling they will find numerous 'new' objects to scrutinize and play with. Packing just one favorite toy is enough, or if there is no favorite toy leave out all of them in favor of stories or imaginary games.

28. CARRY KID FRIENDLY SNACKS

Create a small snack counter in your bag to store away quick bites for those sudden hunger pangs. Depending on the child's age this could include chocolates, raisins, dry fruits, granola bars or biscuits. Also keep a bottle of water handy for your little one.

> TOURIST

These things do not add much weight and can be adjusted in a handbag or knapsack.

29. GAMES TO CARRY

Create some travel specific, imaginary games if you have slightly grown up children, like spot the attractions. Keep a coloring book and colors handy for in-flight or hotel time. Apps on your smart phone can keep the children engaged with cartoons and story books. Older children are often entertained by games available on phones or tablets. This cuts the weight of luggage down while keeping the kids entertained.

30. LET THE KIDS CARRY THEIR LOAD

A good thing is to start early sharing of responsibilities. Let your child pick a bag of his or her choice and pack it themselves. Keep tabs on what they are stuffing in their bags by asking if they will be using that item on the trip. It could start out being just an entertainment bag initially but with growing years they will learn to sort the useful from the superfluous. Children as little as four can maneuver a small trolley suitcase like a pro- their experience in pull along toys credit. If you are worried that you may be pulling it for them, you may want to start with a backpack.

31. DECIDE ON LOCATION FOR CHILDREN TO SLEEP

While on a trip you might not always get a crib at your destination, and carrying one will make life all the more difficult. Instead call ahead to see if there are any cribs or roll out beds for children. You may even put blankets on the floor. Weave them a story about camping and they will gladly sleep without any trouble.

32. GET BABY PRODUCTS DELIVERED AT YOUR DESTINATION

If you are absolutely paranoid about not getting your favourite variety of diaper or brand of baby food, check out online stores like amazon.com for services in your destination city. You can buy things online ahead of your travel and get them delivered to your hotel upon arrival.

33. FEEDING NEEDS OF YOUR INFANTS

If you are travelling with a breastfed infant, you save the trouble of carrying bottles and bottle sanitization kits. For special food, or medications, you may need to call ahead to make sure you have a refrigerator where you are staying.

34. FEEDING NEEDS OF YOUR TODDLER

With the progression from infancy to toddler, their dietary requirements too evolve. You will have to pack some snacks for travelling time. Fresh fruits and vegetables can be purchased at your destination. Most of the cities you travel to in whichever part of the world, will have baby food products and formulas, available at the local drug-store or the supermarket.

35. PICKING CLOTHES FOR YOUR BABY

Contrary to popular belief, babies can do without many changes of clothes. At the most pack 2 outfits per day. Pack mix and match type clothes for your little one as well. Pick things which are comfortable to wear and quick to dry.

36. SELECTING SHOES FOR YOUR BABY

Like outfits, kids can make do with two pairs of comfortable shoes. If you can get some water resistant shoes it will be best. To expedite drying wet shoes, you can stuff newspaper in them then wrap them with newspaper and leave them to dry overnight.

37. KEEP ONE CHANGE OF CLOTHES HANDY

Travelling with kids can be tricky. Keep a change of clothes for the kids and mum handy in your purse or tote bag. This takes a bit of space in your hand luggage but comes extremely handy in case there are any accidents or spills.

38. LEAVE BEHIND BABY ACCESSORIES

Baby accessories like their bed, bath tub, car seat, crib etc. should be left at home. Many hotels provide a crib on request, while car seats can be borrowed from friends or rented. Babies can be given a bath in the hotel sink or even in the adult bath tub with a little bit of water. If you bring a few bath toys, they can be used in the bath, pool, and out of water. They can also be sanitized easily in the sink.

39. CARRY A SMALL LOAD OF PLASTIC BAGS

With children around there are chances of a number of soiled clothes and diapers. These plastic bags help to sort the dirt from the clean inside your big bag.

> TOURIST

These are very light weight and come in handy to other carry stuff as well at times.

PACK WITH A PURPOSE

40. PACKING FOR BUSINESS TRIPS

One neutral-colored suit should suffice. It can be paired with different shirts, ties and accessories for different occasions. One pair of black suit pants could be worn with a matching jacket for the office or with a snazzy top for dinner.

41. PACKING FOR A CRUISE

Most cruises have formal dinners, and that formal dress usually takes up a lot of space. However you might find a tuxedo to rent. For women, a short black dress with multiple accessory options will do the trick.

42. PACKING FOR A LONG TRIP OVER DIFFERENT CLIMATES

The secret packing mantra for travel over multiple climates is layering. Layering traps air around your body creating insulation against the cold. The same light t-shirt that is comfortable in a warmer climate can be the innermost layer in a colder climate.

REDUCE SOME MORE WEIGHT

43. LEAVE PRECIOUS THINGS AT HOME

Things that you would hate to lose or get damaged leave them at home. Precious jewelry, expensive gadgets or dresses, could be anything. You will not require these on your trip. Leave them at home and spare the load on your mind.

44. SEND SOUVENIRS BY MAIL

If you have spent all your money on purchasing souvenirs, carrying them back in the same bag that you brought along would be difficult. Either pack everything in another bag and check it in the airport or get everything shipped to your home. Use an international carrier for a secure transit, but this could be more expensive than the checking fees at the airport.

45. AVOID CARRYING BOOKS

Books equal to weight. There are many reading apps which you can download on your smart phone or tab.

Plus there are gadgets like Kindle and Nook that are thinner and lighter alternatives to your regular book.

CHECK, GET, SET, CHECK AGAIN

46. STRATEGIZE BEFORE PACKING

Create a travel list and prepare all that you think you need to carry along. Keep everything on your bed or floor before packing and then think through once again – do I really need that? Any item that meets this question can be avoided. Remove whatever you don't really need and pack the rest.

47. TEST YOUR LUGGAGE

Once you have fully packed for the trip take a test trip with your luggage. Take your bags and go to town for window shopping for an hour. If you enjoy your hour long trip it is good to go, if not, go home and reduce the load some more. Repeat this test till you hit the right weight.

48. ADD A ROLL OF DUCT TAPE

You might wonder why, when this book has been talking about reducing stuff, we're suddenly asking you to pack something totally unusual. This is because when you have limited supplies, duct tape is immensely helpful for small repairs – a broken bag, leaking zip-lock bag, broken sunglasses, you name it and duct tape can fix it, temporarily.

49. LIST OF ESSENTIAL ITEMS

Even though the emphasis is on packing light, there are things which have to be carried for any trip. Here is our list of essentials:

- Passport/Visa or any other ID

- Any other paper work that might be required on a trip like permits, hotel reservation confirmations etc.

- Medicines – all your prescription medicines and emergency kit, especially if you are travelling with children

- Medical or vaccination records

- Money in foreign currency if travelling to a different country

- Tickets- Email or Message them to your phone

>TOURIST

50. MAKE THE MOST OF YOUR TRIP

Wherever you are going, whatever you hope to do we encourage you to embrace it whole-heartedly. Take in the scenery, the culture and above all, enjoy your time away from home.

On a long journey even a straw weighs heavy.

-Spanish Proverb

>TOURIST

PACKING AND PLANNING TIPS

A Week before Leaving

- Arrange for someone to take care of pets and water plants.
- Stop mail and newspaper.
- Notify Credit Card companies where you are going.
- Change your thermostat settings.
- Car inspected, oil is changed, and tires have the correct pressure.
- Passports and photo identification is up to date.
- Pay bills.
- Copy important items and download travel Apps.
- Start collecting small bills for tips.

Right Before Leaving

- Clean out refrigerator.
- Empty garbage cans.
- Lock windows.
- Make sure you have the proper identification with you.
- Bring cash for tips.
- Remember travel documents.
- Lock door behind you.
- Remember wallet.
- Unplug items in house and pack chargers.

>TOURIST

READ OTHER GREATER THAN A TOURIST BOOKS

Greater Than a Tourist San Miguel de Allende Guanajuato Mexico: 50 Travel Tips from a Local by Tom Peterson

Greater Than a Tourist – Lake George Area New York USA: 50 Travel Tips from a Local by Janine Hirschklau

Greater Than a Tourist – Monterey California United States: 50 Travel Tips from a Local by Katie Begley

Greater Than a Tourist – Chanai Crete Greece: 50 Travel Tips from a Local by Dimitra Papagrigoraki

Greater Than a Tourist – The Garden Route Western Cape Province South Africa: 50 Travel Tips from a Local by Li-Anne McGregor van Aardt

Greater Than a Tourist – Sevilla Andalusia Spain: 50 Travel Tips from a Local by Gabi Gazon

Greater Than a Tourist – Kota Bharu Kelantan Malaysia: 50 Travel Tips from a Local by Aditi Shukla

Children's Book: Charlie the Cavalier Travels the World by Lisa Rusczyk

>TOURIST

> TOURIST

Visit Greater Than a Tourist for Free Travel Tips
http://GreaterThanATourist.com

Sign up for the Greater Than a Tourist Newsletter for discount days, new books, and travel information:
http://eepurl.com/cxspyf

Follow us on Facebook for tips, images, and ideas:
https://www.facebook.com/GreaterThanATourist

Follow us on Pinterest for travel tips and ideas:
http://pinterest.com/GreaterThanATourist

Follow us on Instagram for beautiful travel images:
http://Instagram.com/GreaterThanATourist

>TOURIST

> TOURIST

Please leave your honest review of this book on Amazon and Goodreads. Please send your feedback to GreaterThanaTourist@gmail.com as we continue to improve the series. We appreciate your positive and constructive feedback. Thank you.

>TOURIST

METRIC CONVERSIONS

TEMPERATURE

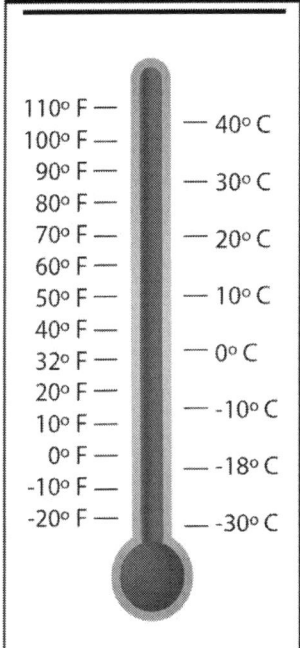

110° F — — 40° C
100° F —
90° F — — 30° C
80° F —
70° F — — 20° C
60° F —
50° F — — 10° C
40° F —
32° F — — 0° C
20° F —
10° F — — -10° C
0° F —
-10° F — — -18° C
-20° F — — -30° C

To convert F to C:

Subtract 32, and then multiply by 5/9 or .5555.

To Convert C to F:
Multiply by 1.8 and then add 32.

32F = 0C

LIQUID VOLUME

To Convert:................Multiply by
U.S. Gallons to Liters................. 3.8
U.S. Liters to Gallons 26
Imperial Gallons to U.S. Gallons 1.2
Imperial Gallons to Liters....... 4.55
Liters to Imperial Gallons 22
1 Liter = .26 U.S. Gallon
1 U.S. Gallon = 3.8 Liters

DISTANCE

To convert ....Multiply by
Inches to Centimeters 2.54
Centimeters to Inches 39
Feet to Meters....................... .3
Meters to Feet 3.28
Yards to Meters 91
Meters to Yards 1.09
Miles to Kilometers 1.61
Kilometers to Miles............ .62
1 Mile = 1.6 km
1 km = .62 Miles

WEIGHT

1 Ounce = .28 Grams
1 Pound = .4555 Kilograms
1 Gram = .04 Ounce
1 Kilogram = 2.2 Pounds

>TOURIST

TRAVEL QUESTIONS

- Do you bring presents home to family or friends after a vacation?
- Do you get motion sick?
- Do you have a favorite billboard?
- Do you know what to do if there is a flat tire?
- Do you like a sun roof open?
- Do you like to eat in the car?
- Do you like to wear sun glasses in the car?
- Do you like toppings on your ice cream?
- Do you use public bathrooms?
- Did you bring your cell phone and does it have power?
- Do you have a form of identification with you?
- Have you ever been pulled over by a cop?
- Have you ever given money to a stranger on a road trip?
- Have you ever taken a road trip with animals?
- Have you ever went on a vacation alone?
- Have you ever run out of gas?

- If you could move to any place in the world, where would it be?
- If you could travel anywhere in the world, where would you travel?
- If you could travel in any vehicle, which one would it be?
- If you had three things to wish for from a magic genie, what would they be?
- If you have a driver's license, how many times did it take you to pass the test?
- What are you the most afraid of on vacation?
- What do you want to get away from the most when you are on vacation?
- What foods smells bad to you?
- What item do you bring on ever trip with you away from home?
- What makes you sleepy?
- What song would you love to hear on the radio when you're cruising on the highway?
- What travel job would you want the least?
- What will you miss most while you are away from home?
- What is something you always wanted to try?

>TOURIST

- What is the best road side attraction that you ever saw?
- What is the farthest distance you ever biked?
- What is the farthest distance you ever walked?
- What is the weirdest thing you needed to buy while on vacation?
- What is your favorite candy?
- What is your favorite color car?
- What is your favorite family vacation?
- What is your favorite food?
- What is your favorite gas station drink or food?
- What is your favorite license plate design?
- What is your favorite restaurant?
- What is your favorite smell?
- What is your favorite song?
- What is your favorite sound that nature makes?
- What is your favorite thing to bring home from a vacation?
- What is your favorite vacation with friends?
- What is your favorite way to relax?

- Where is the farthest place you ever traveled in a car?
- Where is the farthest place you ever went North, South, East and West?
- Where is your favorite place in the world?
- Who is your favorite singer?
- Who taught you how to drive?
- Who will you miss the most while you are away?
- Who if the first person you will contact when you get to your destination?
- Who brought you on your first vacation?
- Who likes to travel the most in your life?
- Would you rather be hot or cold?
- Would you rather drive above, below, or at the speed limited?
- Would you rather drive on a highway or a back road?
- Would you rather go on a train or a boat?
- Would you rather go to the beach or the woods?

>TOURIST

TRAVEL BUCKET LIST

1.

2.

3.

4.

5.

6.

7.

8.

9.

10.